Klever Cavalcanti
Fernando A. Aires Lins

# Improving the security of android mobile devices

Klever Cavalcanti
Fernando A. Aires Lins

# Improving the security of android mobile devices

## An integrated solution for improving the security of mobile devices based on the android platform

ScienciaScripts

**Imprint**



Cover image: www.ingimage.com

This book is a translation from the original published under ISBN 978-3-330-76096-7.

Publisher:
Sciencia Scripts
is a trademark of
Dodo Books Indian Ocean Ltd. and OmniScriptum S.R.L publishing group

120 High Road, East Finchley, London, N2 9ED, United Kingdom
Str. Armeneasca 28/1, office 1, Chisinau MD-2012, Republic of Moldova, Europe
Printed at: see last page
**ISBN: 978-620-8-36359-8**

**Dedication**

I dedicate this work to my wife Andrea, and my daughters Laura and Luana, for the time we missed together. To my parents, Lurdes and Kleber, all credit to them.

## ACKNOWLEDGEMENTS

Firstly to God, for allowing me to get this far, and for giving me strength in difficult times.

Secondly, to the one who is always by my side, at all times and who helps me a lot. Thank you to my wife for always being by my side and helping me in every way, and to my parents for everything they've done and do for me; without them I really wouldn't be realising this dream.

I would like to thank my advisor, professor and friend Fernando Antônio Aires Lins, who really fell out of the sky, a truly human person who knew how to understand the difficulties we go through every day, work and the birth of my daughters, but knew how to charge in a subtle and effective way. I'm very grateful for his achievements, encouragement and generosity.

Thanks also to everyone who directly and indirectly helped a lot in this endeavour, to Professor Gilberto Cysneiros for the *Android* lessons, another wonderful human being, the wisdom and way of conducting things of Professor and Coordinator Tiago Ferreira, Professor Ceça a friend and Professor Rodrigo Assad.

Thank you to the friends I made during my master's degree, I'm very lucky to have met such wonderful and special people, Nielson who was always willing to help, Hélder for his strength and help and all the others who helped a lot.

Epigraph

**"No-one can go back and make a new beginning.**
**But anyone can start again and make a new end."**

**Chico Xavier.**

**SUMMARY**

Nowadays, mobile devices are already part of users' lives, mainly for checking emails, accessing social networks, making payments, accessing bank accounts or surfing the *Internet,* and also because of the need to be connected 24 hours a day. In addition, the number of viruses and attacks by malicious people on mobile devices is growing every day, mainly as a result of behavioural actions by users who don't configure their mobile device correctly, leaving it vulnerable. Actions such as not putting a password on the home screen, not encrypting the memory card, not using an antivirus, downloading unofficial applications and others are examples of user misconfiguration. Therefore, in order to help users configure their mobile devices correctly, this work aims to develop a strategy for minimising security risks on mobile devices. The strategy consists of developing a solution called MSC - *Mobile Security Check,* which aims to help the user search for misconfigurations of the mobile device in terms of security based on 16 pre-configured items in relation to misconfiguration. These 16 items were chosen on the basis of scientific research, articles and security booklets relating to security problems caused by misconfiguration on the part of the end user. This solution was implemented based on the *Android* operating system and is available in this environment's virtual shop. The evaluation of the proposed solution showed that, even with users with a good level of knowledge of security on mobile devices, it is common for there to be a number of configuration vulnerabilities, and the proposed solution works directly to find these loopholes and then publicise them to the end user. In this way, the user is able to take corrective measures to reduce the security risks associated with using the mobile device.
**Keywords:** Mobile devices, Mobile device security, *Android,* user settings.

## SUMMARY

# CHAPTER 1

# INTRODUCTION

The popularisation of mobile devices, such as *tablets, smartphones* and mobile phones, has made mobile devices (especially *smartphones)* a potential target for malicious people. Ordinary users are virtually connected 24 hours a day, whether they're checking *email,* accessing social networks, *Internet banking* or simply surfing the *web*.

According to Grossmann (2015), Brazil is the seventh country in the global ranking in terms of *Internet* use. Another relevant fact, in terms of security, is that by 2016 *malware*, which is any *software* code made with the intention of damaging data, devices or people, will reach 20 million, and 90 per cent of viruses will affect *Android* mobile devices [AVG 2015]. This is due to the fact that *Android* is the most widely used operating system on *smartphones, which means* that the development of malicious code is focussed on this platform [Storn 2014].

Another interesting fact is that in Latin America, Brazil alone accounts for 92.31 per cent of all cases of *ransomware* attacks, which is a type of malicious software *(malware)* that "hijacks" a user's data, i.e. it blocks access to files or systems and, with a payment of a specific amount, releases access to the system. This type of attack has increased in Brazil due to the fact that small and medium-sized businesses have poorly configured equipment, such as simple passwords or no passwords on the mobile device's home screen [Romer 2015].

In addition to *ransomware attacks,* other types of attacks on mobile devices that commonly occur are: SMS attacks, *Bluetooth* attacks, attacks via the public Wi-Fi network where an attacker can intercept traffic (and collect personal data) or divert browsing to fake websites [CERT.br 2013], among others, leaving the mobile device vulnerable to attacks. As well as small and medium-sized businesses having their equipment poorly configured, many users also don't configure their mobile device correctly and end up leaving it with the default configuration, not taking the necessary security precautions (for example, they don't put a password on the home screen, leave *Bluetooth* switched on, don't encrypt the memory card, don't install antivirus software, etc).

Security on mobile devices is a constant concern for users, but even though they are aware of the dangers, they still connect to open WI-FI networks without any security and access bank websites, social networks or emails, leaving themselves vulnerable to attacks by malicious people.

Another point that raises even more concerns is the fact that people use their mobile device on behalf of the company, a concept known as BYOD (*Bring Your Own Device)*, which in free translation means "bring your own device" (D'arcy 2011), greatly increasing the risk of having important or strategic company information accessed by third parties.

There are currently a number of security primers available for users, for example CERT [CERT.br 2013] and CAIS [CAIS/RNP 2012], but users are generally unaware and do not follow basic recommendations, which is why approaches and applications have emerged to check for misconfigurations, which is the main focus of this work.

In summary, it can be said that there is currently a gap in terms of strategies for minimising security risks on Android mobile devices based on the evaluation of high-level user configuration decisions, and especially considering the security guidelines suggested by several important mobile device security references [CERT.br 2013] [CAIS/RNP 2012],

## 1.1 GENERAL OBJECTIVE

This work aims to propose a solution capable of minimising problems related to user misconfiguration on mobile devices. This solution should check the user's mobile device for misconfigurations and then present them to the user with a view to possible corrective actions.

## 1.2 SPECIFIC OBJECTIVES

The main specific objectives of this work are:

- Reduce the risks related to user misconfiguration on the mobile device by checking the mobile device for possible misconfiguration.
- Alert the user to the possibilities of a more secure configuration.
- Providing the proposed solution free of charge to the end user in a virtual shop.
- After the check, it shows the security level of the mobile device (High, Medium or Low).

## 1.3 DEFICIENCIES IN THE STATE OF THE ART

Providing solutions that can minimise security risks on mobile devices is a complex activity when you consider the various possible types of attacks that exist and the vulnerability that mobile devices suffer because users don't have the proper knowledge of how to protect their mobile device.

The authors [Jeter 2013] proposed an application called "Test *Your Phone",* which analyses user behaviour in relation to security when using an *Android* mobile device. In this initiative, this behaviour is analysed through a questionnaire, and the device itself is not evaluated directly, but rather the user's knowledge. Jeter's main contribution is to analyse the data collected from the questionnaire (e.g. it checks whether the user chooses to leave *Bluetooth* enabled, whether the user leaves the GPS feature enabled all the time, among others). However, the initiative does not check the device itself, nor does it allow the user to check and correct any faults.

Another paper that also addresses this issue is [Braga 2012], which presents a case study focussing on vulnerabilities related to modern mobile device platforms. The work shows the problem of user misconfiguration in relation to the mobile device, with emphasis on the issue of the home screen lock password and *rooting* the mobile device. However, the author has not implemented a practical solution that can be installed on mobile devices to detect and correct possible security problems.

Another relevant work is [Vecchiato 2015], in which the authors developed an application to check the security of user settings on mobile devices at different levels, and then this application shows on a single screen the result of the check together with an explanation of how to correct any misconfigured level. There are a total of 14 levels that are checked automatically, and the most relevant levels are: Networks (network information), Passwords (password information), Location (GPS), Applications from Unknown Sources, Antivirus, *Malware* and *Android* version. However, the application doesn't focus on other important points, such as checking that *Bluetooth* is switched on, checking for applications that consume a lot of battery power and overload the device's system. In addition, one of the levels, "Location", only checks whether GPS is switched on; however, another important security issue would be to check applications that use GPS on the *smartphone.*

In summary, these initiatives have addressed and proposed initiatives for mitigating security problems on mobile devices; however, there is a gap in this context regarding an initiative capable of verifying various existing misconfiguration items, where this list of items should be based mainly on existing literature in the area, especially the so-called security primers (which will be covered more fully in Chapter 2).

## 1.4 PROPOSED SOLUTION

In view of the shortcomings of the state of the art described above, this paper presents the MSC - *Mobile Security Check* solution, which aims to analyse the mobile device in order to find possible misconfigurations on the part of the user. The aim of the proposed solution is to minimise the security risks that mobile devices are currently facing. To this end, after checking the mobile device, the solution shows possible security weaknesses and also shows the security level of the mobile device (High, Medium or Low). With this information, it is up to the user to decide whether to follow the recommendation to adopt the most secure settings suggested. To this end, the solution is made up of 16 pre-configured security items related to the user's misconfiguration of the mobile device; these items were drawn up based on research into similar apps on Google Play, security guides, articles and the main mobile device security booklets, especially that of CERT [CERT.br 2014].

The MSC solution differs from other works [Jeter 2013] [Braga 2013] [Thomas 2013] and from existing apps on *Google Play,* such as DU *Battery Saver* [Studio 2015], in that it is aimed at the user's misconfiguration of the mobile device, with items relevant to device security based on official booklets on mobile device security. In addition, the other works that will be shown in this dissertation are generally based on different strategies for a more secure configuration, such as: security questionnaires answered by users and applications that only analyse the type of connection and analyse the device for possible viruses. As a result, the MSC solution actually checks the mobile device for user misconfigurations and recommends a more secure configuration based on 16 items found in the main mobile device security primers, the NIST guidelines [Souppaya 2013] and CERT [CERT.br 2013],

To summarise, the main contribution of this work is the provision of an integrated solution capable of searching for and highlighting possible security risks in mobile devices.

## 1.5 STRUCTURING THE DOCUMENT

In addition to this introductory chapter, this work includes five more chapters, which are briefly described below:

**Chapter 2:** This chapter introduces the basic concepts associated with this work. More specifically, the aspects related to confidentiality, availability, authenticity, access control and the main topics of security primers for mobile devices are described.

**Chapter 3:** In this chapter, a discussion of the work related to this dissertation is presented. These works are discussed and an evaluation of them is made.

**Chapter 4:** This chapter presents the MSC solution for checking possible misconfigurations on *Android* mobile devices. Initially, the chapter presents the functional requirements and the non-functional requirements, as well as showing the comparative study of the items present in current and relevant references in the area. This chapter also presents the solution's architecture and implementation.

**Chapter 5:** In this chapter, which seeks to evaluate the work carried out, various evaluations have been proposed in order to understand and highlight more clearly the contributions of the work and the importance of the proposed solution.

**Chapter 6:** Finally, this chapter presents the conclusions, results achieved and future work associated with this dissertation.

# CHAPTER 2

# BASIC CONCEPTS

When it comes to Information Security, some concepts are fundamental. These concepts are introduced in Section 2.1. Considering the context of this work, which is security in mobile computing, it is also necessary to explain the main references in the area, which will be described in Sections 2.2, 2.3, 2.4 and 2.5 and in 2.6 with final considerations.

## 2.1 FUNDAMENTAL SECURITY ATTRIBUTES

When it comes to security, certain points are considered fundamental, and these are called security attributes. Some of these attributes will be highlighted in this section.

**Confidentiality.** Information must not be made available or disclosed to unauthorised persons, entities or processes. For example, confidential information sent over the *Internet* (e.g. bank passwords) must not be accessed by unauthorised users.

**Availability.** Information must be accessible and usable, even during periods of high demand. For example, the loss of connectivity of a relevant server can affect the availability of the system.

**Integrity.** This consists of protecting information from unauthorised modification, i.e. without the permission of the owners of the information.

**Authenticity.** Guaranteeing that the information is really from the source it claims to be from.

**Access control.** The main objective is to prevent authenticated but unauthorised users from gaining access to a company's system and its functionalities.

## 2.2 ANDROID PLATFORM ARCHITECTURE

*Android* is an open source operating system and platform for mobile devices developed by *Google* and the *Open Handset Alliance* [Alliance 2016], an alliance currently made up of 84 companies, including Google and leading companies in the technology sector. The *Android* platform is subdivided into five main layers, which are:

1) The *Kernel* which is responsible for the core functionalities of the system, such as memory and power management, process management and network protocols optimised for mobile devices [Android 2016].

2) Native Libraries are written in C/C++ and provide basic functionalities that can be accessed by developers through the application *framework* [Android 2016].

3) *Android Runtime* Includes the *Dalvik* virtual machine, designed to be lightweight and have low memory and processing demands, and libraries written in *Java,* which are executed by *Dalvik* [Android 2016].

4) Application *Frameworks* are written in *Java* and provide abstractions of the native libraries, i.e. classes that work together to provide access to the services of these libraries [Android 2016].

5) These are the applications with which users interact directly. They are written in *Java* and each one runs on an independent virtual machine [Android 2016].

## 2.3 ANDROID SECURITY

Fundamental security features that help build secure applications include:

- The Android application sandbox is an effective and simple tool that isolates the execution of programmes and their processes, making it possible to test their operations in a safe and controlled virtual environment.

• An application framework with consistent implementations of common security functionality, such as encryption and permissions;

• An encrypted file system that can be activated to protect data on lost or stolen devices;

• Permissions granted or denied by the user to restrict access to system resources and user data.

## 2.4 MOBILE COMPUTING SECURITY

As we saw in the previous chapter, the growth in the use of mobile devices in recent years is undeniable. And along with this growth, we can see the emergence and growth of risks associated with the use of mobile devices. According to Cavalcanti (2015), these problems/risks can be broadly classified into: loss of the mobile device; insecure communication; use of programmes from suspicious sources; vulnerabilities in the development of mobile applications; and user misconfiguration. These categories are detailed in the following subsections.

### 2.4.1 Loss of mobile device

When a mobile device is lost, not only the *hardware* is compromised, but also its internal information, such as photos, personal documents and settings. For example, a malicious person could plug a USB cable into a *smartphone* and gain access to all the information available on the device. In addition to exposing internal data, a malicious person in possession of this information could demand something in return. Using a password on the home screen and having the memory card encrypted would make it difficult for a malicious person to act on this type of problem [Salutes 2016].

### 2.4.2 Poor communication

Given the large number of places where access to the open (public) WI-FI network is available, many users are unaware of the dangers that can occur when accessing bank accounts, social networks, *e-mails* and *sites* that require the user to enter a *login* and password. More specifically, three points should be analysed in the context of accessing public WI-FI networks: packet captures when accessing *web* pages, obtaining credentials and hijacking accounts or accessing information. For example, a user accessing web pages on a mobile device connected to an open WI-FI network could suffer an attack, considering that a malicious user can check the open network and view all the traffic passing through the network using a *snort,* which is a *Sniffer* (packet capture programme) [CERT.br 2003].

Another concern is if the user uses an application to connect to the mail server (e-mail) without using encryption, thus making it easier for possible *crackers* to access the user's *login* data and/or device.

Account hijacking or access to information doesn't just happen on personal computers, but also on mobile devices. To protect against attacks on data via an open network, it is important to only access networks that use some form of encryption, such as WEP *(Wired Equivalent Privacy),* WPA *^WII^FI Protected Access)* or WEP *(Wired Equivalent Privacy),* the latter being considered the strongest in terms of encryption complexity, and is the one that is currently most widely used [CERT.br 2012],

### 2.4.3 Using Programmes from Suspicious Sources

This category is based on the use of any programmes and applications that are obtained from suspicious sources, or at least not from the *Google Play* shop. Basically, it is not recommended to install applications that are not in the official shops because there is no security check on these applications; in other words, they are not scanned for possible malicious code, in which *malware* may exist. Even so, a considerable number of users make use of programmes from unofficial shops, especially because of the variety of applications available, and are therefore susceptible to attacks. One type of attack known in this context is the *botnet*, known as robots, whose function is to make the mobile device programmed to carry out specific tasks, such as defrauding and deceiving users. To prevent this type of attack, it is best not to *download* applications from unofficial shops and to have an antivirus installed on your mobile device [Braga 2012].

### 2.4.4 Vulnerabilities in mobile application development

Programmes for mobile platforms themselves can be a source of attack risks, as it is common practice for mobile application developers not to worry about or consider existing security risks when designing applications. Three situations will be highlighted in this context: lack of security knowledge on the part of development teams, indirect attacks and applications that require advanced permissions in *Android* [Braga 2012]:

- Insufficient security knowledge on the part of the application development team is a major concern, because many applications are developed on a daily basis without considering basic security concepts and possible tools. Typically, developers create simpler applications without worrying about security in the development process [Braga 2012];
- Another relevant point is the indirect attack, in which *Android* applications have some certificates previously recorded by developers, giving them special access and privileges within the operating system without going through the chain of the certificate validation process. For example, *Adobe* provides certificates for its applications. This process exists to allow other applications to stop using the *Adobe Flash Player plug-in* [Player 2016]. One possible situation is that an attacker can validate a malicious application with a certificate that at first appears to have been validated by *Adobe*'s code, but in fact has not been validated by *Adobe.* Furthermore, while the *Adobe* certificate is present in the application's certificates, the system accepts code released by this application and infects other applications with viruses [Novaes 2014];
- Other risks are associated with application permissions. In order to install an application, the user must accept certain permissions. For example, the user can

install an application that requires his/her permission to use the camera, GPS and other relevant functions. By doing this, the user's mobile device can become more vulnerable, because this application can use these permissions for other purposes that were not mentioned in the installation process. Accepting the request for permissions can even lead to unpleasant consequences, such as misappropriated personal data. The problem becomes even more worrying when permissions are combined, because evaluating all the permissions is stressful and the user usually simply accepts the request without carrying out a meaningful review. One preventative measure is when installing an application to read the permissions and be careful when installing an application that requires a lot of permissions, unless they are considered essential. Unfortunately, it is usually not possible to accept only a subset of these permissions [CAIS/RNP 2012].

#### 2.4.5 User misconfiguration

A considerable number of security attacks are based on the user's lack of knowledge of mobile device security. This type of user is generally not fully aware of what is being done when certain actions are performed on the mobile device. Based on this, this last category is called "User misconfiguration", and it focuses on common user misconfigurations that can produce relevant security risks. As an example, a common configuration error is related to the use of *Bluetooth* and GPS technology. Many users use mobile devices and don't worry about whether *Bluetooth* or GPS are active (even if they don't use them). If *Bluetooth* is active, an attacker can obtain confidential data such as user information without proper consent. In the case of GPS, leaving it always active makes it possible for an attacker to locate the user's current position and use this information against the user's wishes. In addition, these resources being switched on all the time means more energy consumption, which has an impact on the availability of the device [Braga 2012].

Another example of misconfiguration occurs when the user needs to access the *Internet* on their computer and uses the *Internet* on their mobile device. This procedure is known as portable WI-FI router or docking. If not configured correctly, this network is susceptible to attacks in which an attacker can gain access to unauthorised information, i.e. a *smartphone* with an active router function can make it possible, for example, to steal documents, images and video files, install *software* and steal passwords [CAIS/RNP 2012],

Various security problems that can occur on mobile devices have been detailed in this section, all of which can jeopardise the security of mobile devices. However, what was most alarming was user misconfiguration, especially given the large number of risks and misconfigurations commonly found on the *smartphones of* ordinary users (this number will be detailed in the research carried out in Chapter 5), and this fact inspired the development of the solution proposed in this dissertation.

## 2.5 BOOKLETS AND SECURITY GUIDES FOR MOBILE DEVICES

This section shows the main primers on mobile device security that were the basis for developing the solution proposed in this dissertation. An important primer is that of the Centre for the Study, Response and Treatment of Security Incidents in Brazil [CERT.br 2013], which devotes its 14th chapter to security on mobile devices, listing the main security items that must be observed in this context.

Another important booklet is that of the National Research and Educational Network's Security Incident Response Centre [CAIS/RNP 2012], which highlights some important items for mobile device security. And finally, a NIST (Nat/ona/ *Institute of Standards and Technology)* guideline [Souppaya et a/ 2013] shows guidelines for managing mobile device security in companies in order to help organisations centrally manage mobile device security. These references will be briefly described below.

The Mobile Device Security Primer [CERT.br 2013] is divided into 6 topics and 25 subtopics of security that are necessary before purchasing a mobile device. Considering the context of this work, 7 subtopics stand out:

1. **Restoring original settings on used *smartphones*.** When you buy a used mobile device, it's important to restore the original or "factory" settings before you start using it.
2. **Avoid buying a mobile device that has been illegally unlocked.** Known as *jailbreaking*, this practice, as well as being illegal, can breach the warranty terms and jeopardise the security and functioning of the device.
3. **Use an antivirus on the mobile device.** When using a mobile device it is important to install an *anti-malware* programme, for example *Malwarebytes Anti-Malware* [Anti - Malware 2016] before installing any type of application, especially those developed by third parties.
4. **Update the operating system regularly.** It is advisable to always keep the operating system and applications installed at the latest version and with all updates applied.
5. **Avoid installing applications from unknown sources and extensions.** Be careful

when installing applications developed by third parties, such as add-ons and extensions. Try to use applications from reliable sources and that are well rated by users.

**6. Check that the permissions are consistent with the purpose of the application.** We recommend checking that the permissions required for execution are consistent with the application's purpose.

**7. Caution is advised with applications that use social networks with geolocation.** When you log in to a social network, it's important to be careful with geolocation, because it can compromise your privacy and, based on it, it's possible to discover your routine, deduce information (such as habits and financial class) and try to predict your next steps or those of your family members [CERT.br 2013],

Another important booklet is that of the National Research and Educational Network's Security Incident Response Centre [CAIS/RNP 2012], which highlights the need to use an antivirus, but explains that security solutions should not only deal with viruses, but also inhibit the installation of applications that are not from official sources, prevent *rooting*, which is having administrator permissions for the mobile device, and ensure that memory cards are encrypted.

The CAIS/RNP Primer even highlights an entire chapter for *Android* mobile devices, with an emphasis on showing how to access the security settings of any *Android* mobile device. To do this, on any mobile device simply go to the "Security" section of "System Settings" (accessed via the Menu button), where you'll find the operating system's main security settings such as Screen lock and SIM lock. In the screen lock for accessing the mobile device, you can choose the "Password" option, which allows you to set passwords on the device. In SIM lock, you can tick the "Lock SIM card" option and simply click on Change PIN *(Personal Identification Number), which is* a security code that is set on the mobile phone operator's SIM card and is different from the mobile device's lock password. The PIN is already set by the telephone operator, so once it has been changed, only the person who has the password will be able to unlock the SIM card and access the mobile device.

Another relevant reference is the guidelines on mobile device security in companies, produced by NIST (National Institute of Standards and Technology) [Souppaya 2013]. This reference highlights material on Guidelines for Managing Mobile Device Security in Enterprises to help organisations manage mobile device security. It emphasises that mobile devices, such as *smartphones* and *tablets,* usually need to support multiple security objectives such as confidentiality, integrity and availability. To achieve these objectives, mobile devices must be protected against a variety of threats. It also highlights concerns about the public WI-FI network, wireless personal area network interfaces such as *Bluetooth,* and care with GPS activation.

## 2.6 FINAL CONSIDERATIONS

In this chapter, the fundamental security attributes such as Confidentiality, Integrity, Availability and Authenticity were shown. The CERT booklet highlighted 7 security subtopics that are necessary before purchasing a mobile device. The other CAIS/RNP booklet showed security items that are fundamental for correctly configuring a mobile device. The publication of the NIST mobile device security management guidelines is intended to help organisations centrally manage mobile device security. The next chapter presents the work related to the theme of this dissertation.

## CHAPTER 3

## RELATED WORK

This chapter presents the main works that relate in some way to the theme of this dissertation.

### 3.1 DESCRIPTION OF THE INITIATIVES

The first related work to be highlighted in this chapter is [Jeter 2013], whose main idea is to present an analysis of questionnaire data on user behaviour related to security when using *Android* mobile devices. Some of the data analysed is: whether *Bluetooth* is activated, whether the user has *rooted* the mobile device, whether physical needs accessibility features are activated, whether GPS location is activated, among others.

Based on the data collected, the initiative identifies the most significant threats to users, and possible solutions are presented/recommended. Additionally, through a specific application, the work tests the user's security knowledge through questions about the *smartphone*'s functionalities - this functionality is found in the application called "Test *Your Phone",* and is intended to verify possible security flaws arising from the end user's lack of technical knowledge. These flaws are divided into six categories: passwords, text messages and calls, applications, basic *Android* features, permissions and root.

One of the highlights of this work is that it shows the user possible security problems related to the *smartphone*'s configuration, making the mobile device less vulnerable to attacks. Despite this, the work does not actually evaluate the *smartphone* or configure it, which would be an important point, as what the user answers in the questions is not always actually implemented on the mobile device.

In another relevant related work, Braga [Braga 2012] presents a case study regarding the treatment of threats and vulnerabilities related to modern mobile device platforms. In the study carried out on various mobile devices, it was seen that one of the main causes of threats and vulnerabilities is related to poor user configuration. Especially when it comes to controlling access to the mobile device, the case study shows that the user must have a defined password type so that access to the system can be more secure, and in this case *Android* has modes with different levels of security for locking the home screen: 1- Facial

Recognition, 2- Drawing Pattern, 3- Password and 4- PIN *(Personal Identification Number).*

Another point of the case study is in relation to Access Restrictions on the mobile device, in which it explains that *rooting* the mobile device can leave it vulnerable, because the system makes it impossible for the user to install applications with superuser permissions, which would grant such permissions to the application in question [Play 2016].

An important gap in this work is the lack of related items focussed specifically on connection security, which is a relevant item when it comes to mobile device security.

In another relevant initiative, Zefferer [Zefferer 2013] developed an API for analysing mobile device behaviour by evaluating 22 predefined security properties. Some properties stand out in this context, in particular: I) to access the *smartphone,* the user must set a password containing characters and numeric characters, II) check that encryption has been activated, III) check that no alternative keyboard is installed, IV) check that no suspicious application has been registered to receive SMS messages on the device, among others. A negative point of this work is that the API only works via the web, i.e. the user needs to be connected to the *Internet* to perform the check on the mobile device. Another restriction is the limitation of properties, since properties such as: *Bluetooth* enabled, password anchoring, suspicious applications with access to GPS, among others, could also be addressed, which could make the mobile device less vulnerable to other situations or forms of attack.

In another important Vecchiato initiative [Vecchiato 2015], the authors developed an application called "Security Assessment", which aims to help the user check the mobile device's settings at different security levels. The application basically assesses the security of *Android* devices based on the settings defined by users.

This application extracts 14 security levels automatically, and these levels are based on the user's mobile device settings. The information about these settings is sent to an external web service, which contains a pre-defined list of security for each level in order to compare the levels collected on the mobile device with a list. For example, in the list contained in the web service, the "antivirus" level contains a database with the following information: two lists of *malware,* the first extracted from the *Malgenome* project [ZhouY 2012] which provides a large collection of 1.260 *Android malware* and the other list created based on an in-depth search for security applications on *Google Play* and various developer forums, for example [xdadevelopers 2016] and [stackoverow 2016]; after extracting the data, the web service returns a response to the user, and this response contains the "result" that shows which levels need to be fixed and "how to fix". The main levels proposed in the application are: Networks (which checks for network problems such as whether any encryption is being used), Location (checking whether GPS is switched on), Unknown Sources (use of unofficial apps from the *Google Play* shop) and Antivirus (checking for possible *malware* on the mobile device).

The proposed application helps the user to have a more secure configuration and prevent the risks of misconfiguration, but it could focus on other more specific configurations such as: checking memory card encryption, checking that *Bluetooth* is switched on, checking applications that consume a lot of battery and checking applications that overload the device in terms of processing. In addition, at the "Location" level, the application only checks that GPS is switched on; however, it would also be important to check for applications that use GPS without permission.

## 3.2 COMPARATIVE DISCUSSION

In view of the work presented, it can be said that [Jeter 2013] and [Braga 2012] focused on analysing user behaviour, one of the points being the *Test Your Phone* application, which only tests security knowledge by asking questions about the *smartphone*'s functionalities, and it is known that what the user answers does not always match in practice.

Another important point is that there was a lack of focus on relevant applications that are necessary for user misconfiguration, such as checking the encryption of the memory card, checking that it is switched on, checking applications that consume a lot of battery and checking applications that overload the device in terms of processing.

On the other hand, other initiatives [Zefferer 2013] and [Vecchiato 2015] have proposed checking the user's mobile device in real time for possible security breaches due to misconfiguration by the user. This approach proved to be more interesting, as the fact that the user has security knowledge does not always mean that they will configure the device in a less risky way (this fact will also be shown in the evaluation chapter of this work).

However, these initiatives focussed on specific security problems, and were not explicitly based on any of the important primers explained in Chapter 2; therefore, important points such as: *Bluetooth* is switched on, checking applications that consume a lot of battery, checking applications that overload the device in terms of processing, password docking, suspicious applications with access to GPS and others related to user misconfiguration ended up not being addressed in these initiatives.

## 3.3 FINAL CONSIDERATIONS

This section presents the main works related to the subject proposed in this dissertation, and after analysing them it was possible to see that there is a gap in terms of a solution for assessing user misconfigurations that is based on widely adopted security guidelines or references (such as those explained in Chapter 2).

A comparative discussion of these initiatives is also provided. The next chapter presents the MSC solution, which was proposed with a view to filling this gap.

## CHAPTER 4

# MOBILE SECURITY CHECK: A SOLUTION FOR IMPROVING THE SECURITY OF *ANDROID* MOBILE DEVICES

The overall aim of this work is to develop a solution that can mitigate security problems arising from misconfigurations by users on mobile devices.

In other words, a strategy that can check, report and classify possible settings on mobile devices by the user that pose security risks to the device and the sensitive data stored on it.

The security basis associated with this work was drawn up by researching articles and security primers from NIST [Souppaya *et al* 2013] and CERT [CERT.br 2013], both of which were discussed in Chapter 2.

This solution was implemented based on the *Android* operating system, as it is the most widely used and most targeted by malicious people [Storn 2014] and is currently available in the virtual shop associated with this operating system. This chapter is structured as follows. Section 4.1 discusses the MSC Solution Requirements. Section 4.2 details the MSC architecture, section 4.3 shows the solution overview, section 4.4 the implementation and section 4.5 final considerations.

## 4.1 REQUIREMENTS

This section details the functional and non-functional requirements considered for the development of the proposed solution. In particular, the functional requirements were taken from relevant references on the subject, especially the [CERT.br 2013] security booklet, the [CAIS/RNP 2012] booklet, the Information and Computer Systems Security mini-course at the XII Brazilian Symposium on Information and Computer Systems Security (SBSEG) [Braga 2012] and the NIST recommendations guide [Souppaya and Scarfone 2013]. This led to a comparative study of the most important functional security items on mobile devices, which are described in Table 4.1.

**Table 4.1- Comparative study of the items in the basic references**

| Functional Items | CERT Primer | CAIS booklet | SBSEG | NIST |
|---|---|---|---|---|
| 1. SMS files (Short Message Service ) stored on the mobile device | X | X | X | |
| 2. Cautions when using public WI-FI networks | X | X | X | X |
| 3. *Jailbreak* or *Root* | X | | X | |
| 4. Use an antivirus | X | X | | |
| 5. *Bluetooth* disabled | X | | | X |
| 6. Installing applications from unsafe sources | X | X | X | X |
| 7. Avoid suspicious applications that use GPS | X | X | | X |
| 8. Keep sensitive information in encrypted format at all times | X | X | X | X |
| 9. Screen lock | X | X | X | X |
| 10. Applications with high data plan consumption | | X | X | |
| 11. Applications that demand a lot of processing | | X | X | |
| 12. Applications with high battery consumption | | X | X | |
| 13. Existence of a P2P connection | X | | | |
| 14. Password anchoring | X | | X | |
| 15. Quality of the anchor bolt | X | | X | |
| 16. Security of trafficked data | X | X | | X |
| 17. Suspicious applications with access to the diary | X | X | | |
| 18. Loss of mobile device | X | | X | |
| 19. Verify digital signatures in applications | | | | X |

*The* comparative study shows that items 1- "SMS (Short Message Service) files stored on the mobile device", 2- "Take care when using public WI-FI networks", 6- "Install applications from unsecured sources", 8- "Always keep sensitive information in encrypted format" and 9- "Screen lock", in the comparison of functional items, were the ones that were present in all the references, due to the fact that they are the most vulnerable when it comes to misconfiguration of the mobile device by the user. They are therefore automatically included in the solution's functional requirements, which will be explained in the next subsection, 4.1.1.

Other items such as: 4- Use an antivirus, 5- *Bluetooth* disabled, 6- Install applications from unsafe sources, 7- Avoid suspicious applications that use GPS and 8- Always keep sensitive information in encrypted format.

### 4.1.1 Functional requirements

This subsection details the functional requirements considered for the development of the proposed solution.

**[RF 01] Check that the device's screen lock password is set.** If the mobile device is lost or stolen, using a lock password will make it more difficult to tamper with the data stored on the mobile device. In addition, it is important to check that a password with numbers and/or letters is used, as the finger swipe method is not considered secure, since by placing the mobile device against the light anyone can see the outline where the swipe was made.

**[RF 02] Search for installed applications obtained from unofficial sites.** Installing applications from trusted sources, such as official shops, reduces the possibility of viruses or malicious code.

**[RF 03] Check that the memory card is encrypted.** The importance of this check is due to the fact that an unencrypted memory card makes sensitive data more likely to be tampered with by malicious people.

**[RF 04] Check for applications with access to reading SMS.** Every application that is installed asks for permission to access various features of the mobile device, so it is important to make sure that the application actually has the permissions it needs. In particular, a malicious application with access to reading the user's SMS could take advantage of this access to carry out attacks or send messages without the user's permission.

**[RF 05] Check that the user has activated Internet docking/routing using a password.** It is common for users to configure their mobile device as a router *for Internet* sharing. However, routing the WI-FI signal without a password leaves the mobile device vulnerable to attack by malicious people.

**[RF 06] Check that the password used for *Internet* anchoring is weak.** Using a weak password is when you don't have a combination of letters, numbers and characters, and it's essential to avoid using it to make it more difficult for malicious people to access the mobile device.

**[RF 07] Search for applications that have access to the GPS feature.** There are malicious applications that request permission to access GPS without even needing it, which is a risk for the user, as a malicious person could activate it and the user's location could be sent to an unknown recipient.

**[RF 08] Check whether a P2P connection is being used.** With this type of connection, it is difficult to know the origin of the file being downloaded. It is also difficult to ascertain whether or not a file is secure.

**[RF 09] Check if there are any applications with access to the mobile device's address book.** In theory, only text messaging applications, social networks and contact books use the device's address book. It is important to warn the user that other applications also use it.

**[RF 10] Check that the Bluetooth connection is activated.** Active Bluetooth leaves the mobile device vulnerable to attacks or information theft via the wireless connection. In addition, active *Bluetooth* causes unnecessary energy consumption that could be avoided, degrading the mobile device's battery charge.

**[RF 11] Check that the WI-FI connection is using a security mechanism.** Using an encrypted connection makes sensitive data less susceptible to network attacks, especially interception and tampering.

**[RF 12] Search for suspicious (malicious) applications.** Applications with malicious or malicious code can carry out various types of attacks on users' mobile devices, most notably the man-in-the-middle attack [Grossmann 2014], in which the malicious person stands in the middle of the user's *Internet* connection and can thus intercept the connection data, and this data exchanged between two parties can be manipulated.

**[RF 13] The solution should check that the user uses a recommended antivirus.** The use of antivirus is traditionally suggested in computing. In this case, the solution should check whether a "recommended" antivirus is being used; if not, the solution suggests using 11 antiviruses with the best scores in usability, performance and protection and which are aimed at *Android* mobile devices, according to the study by [AV-TEST, 2016]. Some of the criteria evaluated to choose the 11 best antiviruses are: "Detection of the latest *Android malware* discovered in the last 4 weeks", in the protection section. In performance, the criteria were: "The app does not affect battery life", "The app does not slow down the device during normal use", "The app does not generate too much traffic" and others. The usability criteria adopted were "block calls from specific or unknown numbers", Protection from malicious websites and/or against *phishing*. Locate, lock or erase your device when it's lost or stolen and others.

**[RF 14] The solution should look for and highlight applications that consume the most data.** Often some applications consume more than expected, even if they are not used by the user very often, and the user's data plan can be exhausted, leading to unavailability of the connection.

**[RF 15] Search for and highlight the applications that overload the mobile device's processor the most.** Overloading the system as a whole slows down the device, often leading to momentary or lasting unavailability. It is important for the user to be aware of the applications installed on the mobile device that contribute to this.

**[RF 16] Look out for applications that consume a lot of energy.** Applications that fall into this category not only reduce battery life, but also make the mobile device unavailable more quickly.

### 4.1.2 Non-functional requirements

This subsection will detail the non-functional requirements considered for the development of the proposed solution.

**[RNF 01] The solution must endeavour to provide security for the data it transmits.** As it is a security application, it is desired that the proposed solution communicates securely when it needs to send user data over insecure networks (e.g. the Internet) and makes requests in the external environment.

## 4.2 SOLUTION OVERVIEW

Based on the functional and non-functional requirements described in the previous section, a solution called *Mobile Security Check* (MSC) was developed so that mobile devices have more secure configurations/decisions regarding mobile device security. This section presents an overview of the solution. More specifically, Figure 4.1 shows the main components of this solution and the steps required to run it.

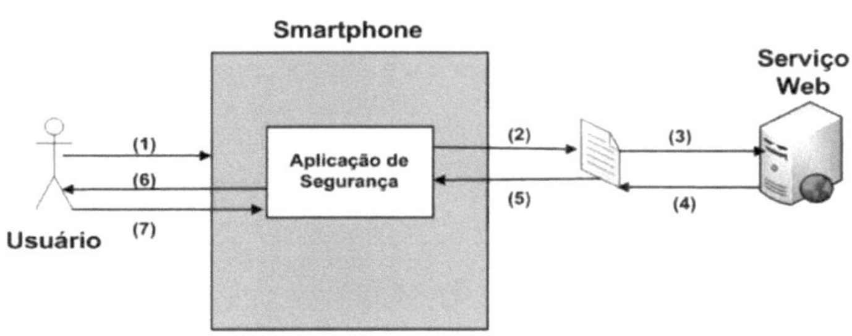

**Figure 4.1-Overview of the proposed solution**

From a general point of view, the solution is installed on the user's *smartphone* and communicates via the *Internet* with a web service to obtain external security information.

The main idea is that only the "Malicious and/or suspicious applications" security item uses the *Internet* to access the Web service, so that the user doesn't have to rely on it alone to carry out the check due to bad device settings and also so as not to overload the mobile device with synchronisation with the Web service, so the others look for the information internally on the mobile device, and if there is no Internet connection at the time of the check, the MSC will postpone the check of the item that requires the Web service and then the user will have to carry out the check again on the mobile device.

The steps required to implement the solution proposed in this work are shown in Figure 4.1.

1- **User initialises the application.** In this step, the user interacts directly with the MSC solution and starts the security check.

2- **The MSC solution evaluates the user's mobile device.** In this step, the check is made internally for possible user misconfigurations based on 16 predefined items, which are directly linked to the requirements presented in Section 4.1.

Each of these 16 items is summarised and described below in Table 4.2.

**Table 4.2- The 16 items of the MSC solution**

| | Items | Description |
|---|---|---|
| I | Password on the home screen | Check that the user has set a password on the Start screen. |
| II | Memory Card Encryption | Check that the memory card is encrypted. |
| III | Existence of applications with access to SMS reading | List applications that have access to SMS reading. |
| IV | Password anchoring | Show if the user has set a password on the dock (WI-FI Router). |
| V | Quality of the anchor bolt | Inform the user if the Anchor password is weak. |
| VI | Applications with GPS access | List applications with permission to the device's GPS feature. |
| VII | Existence of a P2P connection | Show if the device is using P2P *(Peerto Peer)* connections. |
| VIII | Applications with access to the diary | List applications with access to the mobile device's diary. |
| IX | *Bluetooth* active | Inform the user if *Bluetooth* is active. |

| X | Applications installed from an unknown source | Show the user applications that are not from the *Google Play* shop. |
|---|---|---|
| XI | Secure WI-FI connection | Indicate whether WPA2 encryption is being used for the WI-FI connection |
| XII | Existence of suspicious applications | Search the Web Service for applications considered suspicious. |
| XIII | Recommended antivirus installed | Suggest the use of the most recommended antivirus, according to the [AV-TEST 2016] study, for mobile devices. |
| XIV | Applications with high data plan consumption | Show the user which applications consume the most data available on the device. |
| XV | Applications that demand a lot of processing | Show the user which applications overload the mobile device's processing. |
| XVI | Applications with high battery consumption | Show the user applications with high battery consumption. |

3- **The MSC solution sends a request to the Web Service.** In this step, the Web Service receives a request from the solution in order to check for possible suspicious and/or malicious applications. This information is sent securely, using SSL encryption to guarantee confidentiality. This web service contains an extensive list of applications already classified as malicious by CERT (Centre for the Study, Response and Treatment of Security Incidents). This list contains applications that have already been classified as malicious code, for example, for not validating the SSL (Secure *Socket Layer)* certificate [Grossmann 2014], for impairing the performance of the mobile device and for stealing information, and is updated automatically by CERT every thirty days and manually by the solution developer on a daily basis. SSL is a protocol developed to increase the security of data transmitted over the *Internet* and without SSL the mobile device may be more vulnerable to the attack known as *Man-in-the-middle, a* common attack to steal information [Grossmann 2014].

4- **The web service forwards the response to the mobile device.** In this step, after comparing the user's list of applications with the list of malicious applications, the web service forwards a response listing possible malicious applications or the message "There are no suspicious (malicious) applications".

5- **The result reaches the mobile device.** In this step, the solution, in possession of the response from the web service, integrates the results together with the results of the 15 internal check items, totalling 16 items. At this point, the solution will check the security level of the mobile device (Low, Medium or High).

6- **The solution shows the classification of the Security level the mobile device is at and provides suggestions for improving the configuration.** In this step, the solution shows the user what security level their mobile device is at (Low, Medium or High) and also provides suggestions on how to improve, eliminate or mitigate the security risks found.

In view of the various items in Table 4.2, a table was drawn up to measure the degree of severity of the event for the user. This severity can be described using the equation severity = probability of occurrence x associated impact. The probability relates to the likelihood of the event occurring and the associated impact quantifies the extent of the damage caused by the event. This equation was inspired by the PMBOK (Pro/ect *Management Body of Knowledge)* [PMBOK 2014], which suggests techniques for valuing risks. Table 4.3 illustrates the context explained.

**Table 4.3 - Quantification of safety items**

| Category: | Safety items |
|---|---|
| Probability | (1) Low (2) Medium (3) High |
| Impact | (1) Low (2) Medium (3) High |
| Gravity | = Probability x Impact |
| If the Severity varies from: 1 and 2-Low Risk<br>3 and 4-Medium Risk<br>6 and 9-High Risk | |

The functional items "Home screen with password", "There are applications with access to GPS", "Memory card is not encrypted" and "Applications that consume a lot of battery" were present in 3 or more of the basic references in the comparative study described in Table 4.1 and also due to the risk caused to the user by the poor configuration of these items, they formed the "High" severity level.

The functional items that were present in 2 references and posed a moderate risk to the user due to misconfiguration formed the "Medium" level and the items "WI-FI connection is secure (WPA2)", "Applications that consume the most of the data plan", "There are applications with access to reading SMS", "There is no P2P (Peer to Peer) connection" and "There are applications with access to the diary" present in 2 references, but with a low risk to the user and which are not related to user misconfiguration form the "Low" severity items. Table 4.4 shows the distribution of security items with their respective severity level.

**Table 4.4- Safety items with their respective severity level**

| **Safety items** | **Severity Level** |
|---|---|

| | |
|---|---|
| Home screen with password | High |
| There are apps with GPS access | High |
| Memory card is not encrypted | High |
| Battery-hungry apps | High |
| You don't have a recommended antivirus installed | Medium |
| *Bluetooth* is activated | Medium |
| Your anchor (Routing WI-FI) has a password | Medium |
| Your anchor (Routing WI-FI) has a weak password | Medium |
| There are suspicious (malicious) applications | Medium |
| Applications installed from an unknown source | Medium |
| Applications that overload the *Android* system | Medium |
| WI-FI connection is secure (WPA2) | Bass |
| Applications that consume the most data | Bass |
| There are applications with access to SMS reading | Bass |
| No P2P *(Peer to Peer)* connection | Bass |
| There are apps with access to the diary | Bass |

7- **The user interacts with the mobile device.** In this step, the user clicks on each item on the mobile device which will display an alert to the user with tips on how to correct any security flaws.

The final assessment of the mobile device's Security level rating can be Low, Medium or High according to the following considerations:

1- With regard to user misconfiguration, a mobile device that has the result of two low-level security items marked with an "X" as shown in figure 4.3 will be classified as having a high level of security;

2- If there are no security items marked with an "X" in the Low level classification, but there are two Medium security items marked, the mobile device will be classified as Medium;

3- If two or more High level security items are marked with an "X", MSC will automatically classify them as low level security.

## 4.3 MSC ARCHITECTURE

The architecture is the definition of elements such as classes and components and how they relate to each other within the MSC solution.

The following are the classes for the initialisation of the solution's screen by the user: the first is the class for checking the mobile device, the second class is access to the web service and the classes for the mobile device's security level.

1- "Start check" used the "Ma/nAct/v/ty" class.

2- After initialisation, the "order/ncafegory" and "showAsAcf/on" classes are responsible for the solution's start screen.

3- The classes new *ProgressesDialog* (v.Getcontext) to display the message to the user "Loading"; "Wait a bit".

4- Also on the home screen, other important classes for building the solution's home screen are "ListaVulnerabilidadesAcf/v/fy.class", "ListaSobre.*class*" and "ListaAjuda2.*class"*.

5- Through the "message" class, a request is sent to the Web Service. More details in section 4.2 in Solution Overview.

An overview of the solution's class diagram can be seen in figure 4.2.

6-

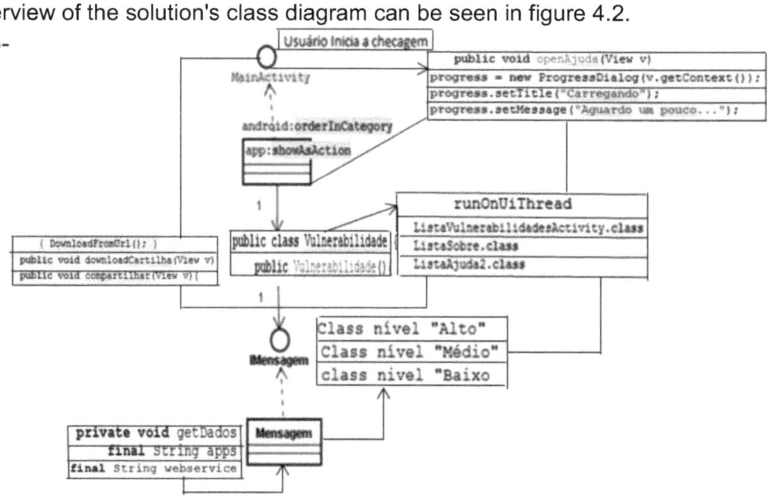


**Figure 4. 2- Class diagram of the solution**

6- After the "message" class sends the request to the web service, the getData class compares it with the web service's list and sends the response to the user using the "message" class.

Other Android classes used to check the solution's security items on the user's mobile device will be described below:

- The InitialPassword class searches for the *lockpatternutils* class and uses one of its methods to check whether or not the mobile device's screen is locked. If it doesn't find the *" Class. forName"("com. android. internai. widget. LockPattern Utils"* or if it gives an error afterwards it means that the lock screen is not implemented or is not working, i.e. in this case the user has not set a password on the home screen.
- Another class *"AppsPermisaaoGps(ConSext context)"* creates a list of installed apps for each app and queries the app's permissions in order to check whether there is permission to access the *coarse* (via approximate positioning by satellite transmission) or fine (GPS) code. The *"access point"* class was used to check that the password is set on the mobile device.
- *the "apmaaager"* class checks if the password is less than 6 digits long or if it has the characters needed to build a strong password.

## 4.4 IMPLEMENTATION

The free *Android* Studio 2.0 tool [Studio 2016] and JDK 7 (Java Development Kit 7) [Oracle 2016] were used to create the MSC solution. MSC supports *Android* mobile devices with versions 4.0 to 6.0.

In terms of user interface, the MSC solution basically consists of 4 screens. The main screen has the following functions: starting the device's security check, providing general information about the solution via the "Help" and "About the Application" items, sharing the solution and finally presenting the CERT security booklet so that the user can clarify any doubts.

The second screen of the MSC details the "Help" item, which explains how to use the solution. The third screen shows information on the "About the application" item, which describes the solution's features. Finally, the fourth screen shows all 16 items related to user misconfiguration and the classification of the security level of the user's mobile device, as shown in Figure 4.3.

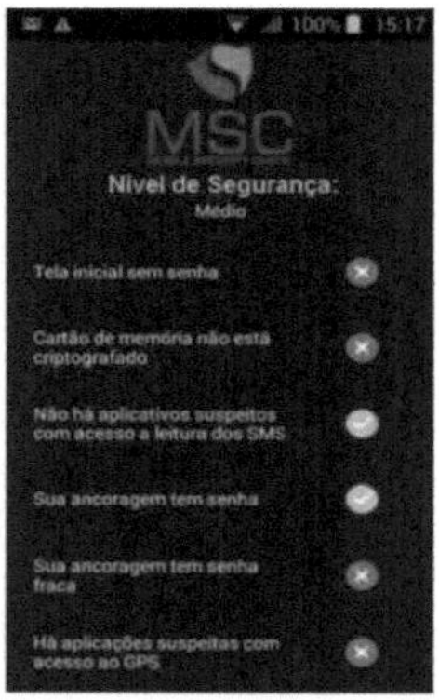


**Figure 4. 3- Security level classification**

The user can select one of the items, and the MSC solution is able to provide information relating to this item. For example, in the case of the item "There are suspicious applications with access to GPS", the MSC provides the answer illustrated in Figure 4.4.

**Figure 4.4- MSC screen showing applications with GPS permissions**

Some of the security items such as: Home screen with password, Memory card is not encrypted, *Bluetooth* is not activated, Your anchor (Route WI-FI) has password and Your anchor (Route WI-FI) has weak password were implemented using resources and information available on the user's own *smartphone*. An important decision was to show that the MSC can also search for information in a list of malicious applications outside the application, using a secure web service and thus making the application more dynamic, as it only needs to update the list of insecure applications in the web service, avoiding the need to update the version of the application itself. An example of an item that is checked using only the user's device resources is checking the type of authentication for the wireless network (WI-FI) that is being used. Examples of possible connections are: WEP (W/red *Equivalent Privacy),* WPA (W/-F/ *Protected Access)* and WPA2 (W/-F/ *Protected Access //)* [Dermatine 2013], and these can be checked internally using the code below.

```
        fc.controller().getBaixo().WifiSecurityLevel(this) a variável
WifiSecurity recebe o valor do método WifiSecurityLevel que tem a
função de mostrar qual tipo de conexão o dispositivo móvel apresenta.

          (1) int WifiSecurity =
  fc.controller().getBaixo().WifiSecurityLevel(this);

          String conexao = "";
          switch (WifiSecurity) {
              case (3): {
                  conexao = "WPA2";
                  break;
              }
              case (2): {
                  conexao = "WPA";
                  break;
              }
              case (1): {
                  conexao = "WEP";
                  break;
              }
              case (0): {
      conexao = "Aberto";
                  break;
              }
          }
```

Access to the web service works as follows: firstly, the mobile device is scanned for installed applications; after this activity, the list of applications is sent to the web service in order to compare the installed applications with the list of malicious applications and thus return a message to the mobile device whether or not it has a malicious application, as shown in code (2).

```
private void getDados(){
        final String apps = fc.controller().getAlto().Apps(ListaVulnerabilidadesActivity.this);
    final String webservice = http://mercuriosi.com/webservice/api/Aplicativos
            new Thread() {
                public void run()
                    try {
                     String pg = "package="+apps;
                     String Url = webservice;
                    final String retorno = Util.getData(pg, Url);
```

Finally, some of the items in Table 4.2 will be described at this point. In the case of the item "You don't have a recommended antivirus installed", it works as follows: within the application there is a list of the 11 best antiviruses based on the evaluation of the AV-TEST company [AV- TEST 2016], which tests antiviruses considering their usability and protection. If the user's antivirus is not among those recommended, the user is notified so that they can make a change.

In the items "Apps that overload the *Android* system*",* "Apps that consume the most data" and "Apps that consume a lot of battery", two classifications were created:

I- Applications with high battery consumption are analysed on the basis of information from the *Android* Operating System itself and added to a predetermined list that the MSC has available, taken from the *Android pit* website [Serowy 2015], and the user is shown the two results.

II- Applications that overload the *Android* system and consume the most data are analysed by a predetermined list that the MSC solution provides. With regard to item II, sometimes a user may have a specific application that traditionally consumes a lot (for example, the data network), but because that user doesn't use the application very much, it doesn't end up presenting this problem in practice. The study was based on a report by AVG (Antivirus Guard) [Serowy 2016] which, every quarter, prepares a report based on data collected from millions of mobile devices around the world and publishes its list of the apps that consume the most energy.

## 4.5 FINAL CONSIDERATIONS

This chapter has described the main contribution of this work, which is a solution for improving the security settings that users make on their mobile devices. This solution, implemented through an application called *Mobile Security Check,* helps to mitigate security problems caused by poor user settings. The next chapter presents the evaluations that were carried out in order to better understand the contribution of the solution proposed in this dissertation.

**CHAPTER 5**

# EVALUATION

The purpose of this chapter is to evaluate the solution proposed in this work. To this end, four evaluations were carried out. The first evaluation consists of installing the MSC solution on two groups of users and then checking the security of their *smartphones.* The second seeks to assess the level of understanding/interest in mobile device security among users of these *smartphones.*

In the third evaluation, the aim is to compare the data collected in the first and second evaluations, in order to check whether users who have an understanding of or interest in security tend to adopt good configuration policies.

Finally, the fourth evaluation seeks to show the level of energy consumption of the MSC solution on the mobile device, in order to assess whether it is energy efficient; this is important because the MSC solution itself suggests using applications that have a satisfactory level of energy consumption.

## 5.1 EVALUATION OF THE EXECUTION OF THE MSC SOLUTION ON SMARTPHONES

The aim of this evaluation is to install and run the MSC solution on the *smartphones of* two groups of users, each with 25 users, of both sexes, aged between 15 and 60, who downloaded the MSC solution via *Google Play.* The first group was selected because it has IT (Information Technology) expertise and the other group of users, a priori, has no IT expertise.

We chose to separate these two different groups to show that even IT-savvy users eventually make insecure configuration decisions. The groups downloaded the MSC solution via *Google Play.*

In this case, the MSC solution checked the pre-defined security items on the *smartphones of* these two groups, and found that they all had a relatively high percentage of mobile device misconfigurations, as shown in Table 5.1.

**Table 5.1- Percentage of misconfigurations in the *smartphones* evaluated**

| Items analysed | Users IT | Non-IT users |
|---|---|---|
| Memory card is not encrypted | 86% | 94,1% |
| Home screen without password | 72% | 86% |
| Anchoring (WI-FI router) has no password | 70% | 90% |
| Existence of applications with access to the diary | 92% | 82,4% |
| Existence of applications with access to GPS | 85% | 70,6% |
| Anchor (WI-FI router) has a weak password | 78% | 94% |
| Existence of applications with access to SMS reading | 81% | 70,6% |
| No P2P connection | 96% | 94,1% |
| *Bluetooth* activated | 8% | 17,6% |
| Applications installed other than from the official Google Play shop | 84% | 76,5% |
| WI-FI connection is not secure (use of encryption) | 100% | 100% |
| No suspicious applications | 96% | 94,1% |
| No recommended antivirus | 46,5% | 63,50% |
| High battery consumption applications | 100% | 100% |
| Existence of applications that overload the *Android* system | 96% | 94,2% |
| High mobile data consumption | 94,5% | 94,1% |

Looking at the results shown in Table 5.1, one can understand more precisely the importance of the solution proposed in this work, mainly because users in general don't configure or don't bother to configure their *smartphone* correctly, since a large percentage of risk occurrences were found in critical situations. For example, a considerable number of users in both groups do not encrypt the memory card. Another example is that, of the users with IT knowledge, only 28 per cent use a password on the home screen and 86 per cent don't encrypt the memory card; in the case of users without IT knowledge, the data is more worrying, as 94 per cent use anchoring (WI-FI routing) with a weak password and 86 per cent of users use a home screen without a password. With the use of the MSC solution, it is possible for the user to realise these points of failure; after visualising and evaluating possible actions/solutions, the user can act to improve the *smartphone's* security configuration.

## 5.2 ASSESSING USERS' LEVEL OF UNDERSTANDING OF MOBILE COMPUTING SECURITY

Using the same set of users who had installed the MSC solution, another evaluation was carried out to address security issues on *Android* mobile devices. To this end, a questionnaire was drawn up with questions on mobile device security and on some of the items in the security booklets presented earlier in this paper. The result of this enquiry is shown in Table 5. 2

**Table 5. 2- Users' level of understanding**

| Questions | Responses from IT users | | Response from non-IT users | |
|---|---|---|---|---|
| | Yes | No | Yes | No |
| Do you have a computer qualification? | 44,2% | 55,8% | 11% | 89% |
| Does it encrypt the memory card? | 38,3% | 61,7% | 6% | 94% |
| Sh are Internet with a password? | 76,7% | 23,3% | 22,5% | 77.5% |
| *Bluetooth* activated | 18% | 82% | 73,8% | 26,2% |
| Do you use WI-FI with encryption? | 51,2% | 48,8% | 9% | 91% |
| Do you have antivirus software? | 68,5% | 31,5% | 36,5% | 63,5% |

Another important point is the type of screen lock used, as it is known that a mobile device without a password or with a simpler type of lock makes it easier for unauthorised users to access sensitive data.

According to Braga [Braga 2012], the ideal would be to use a password and a PIN for greater security, because many users set a weak password. In addition, the use of the "swipe" type of lock is known to be insecure, as an attacker can see a trace on the device's screen of the pattern/drawing that is always done by the user. Figure 5.1 shows a graph with the results of the questionnaire relating to which type of screen lock is most used by users with TL knowledge

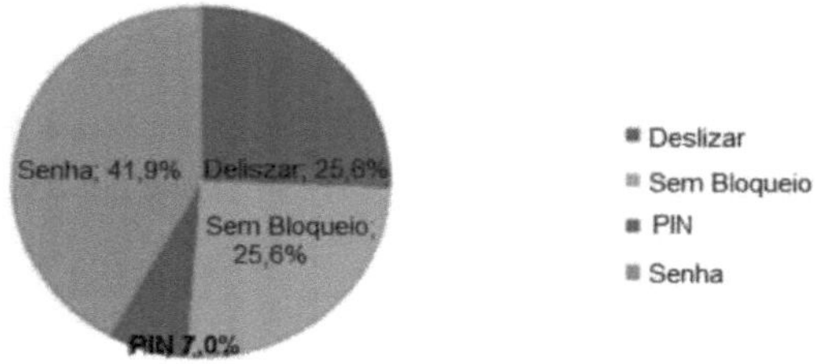

**Figure 5.1- Type of IT user blocking**

In turn, Figure 5.2 shows the results of the questionnaire relating to which type of screen lock is most used by users without IT knowledge.

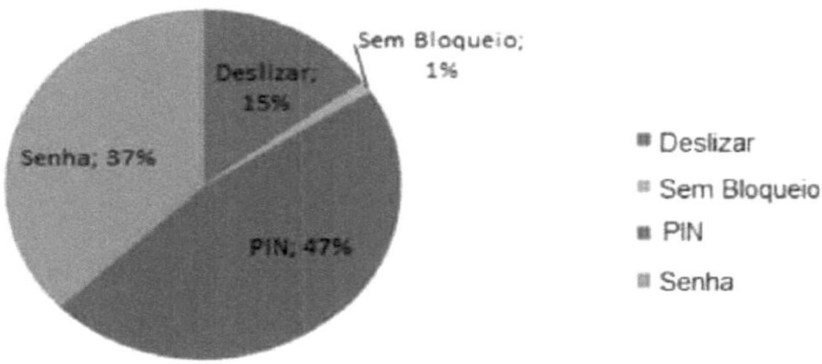


**Figure 5.2- Type of blocking by users without in-depth IT knowledge**

The results show that even with IT knowledge and possibly the security risks of poorly configured mobile devices, many users do not configure their *smartphone* correctly. Some of the items in Table 5.2 stand out, such as the item "*Bluetooth* activated" with 73.8 per cent for users without IT knowledge, the fact that 61.7 per cent of users with IT knowledge do not encrypt the memory card and 91 per cent of users without IT knowledge enter the WI-FI network without encryption. In addition, more specifically, Figure 5.1 shows that of the four types of password settings, only 41.9 per cent of IT users put a password on the home screen and Figure 5.2 shows that only 15 per cent of "non-IT" users use the "password" lock type on the home screen; these figures are relevant and raise concerns about the security of mobile devices, especially considering the possibility of theft of the physical device.

## 5.3 BENCHMARKING

The main objective of the comparative evaluation is to check whether, even if they are aware of security, users in general make the right decisions regarding the device's security policies. To do this, the data obtained in the two previous evaluations is cross-referenced and can be seen in Figure 5.3.

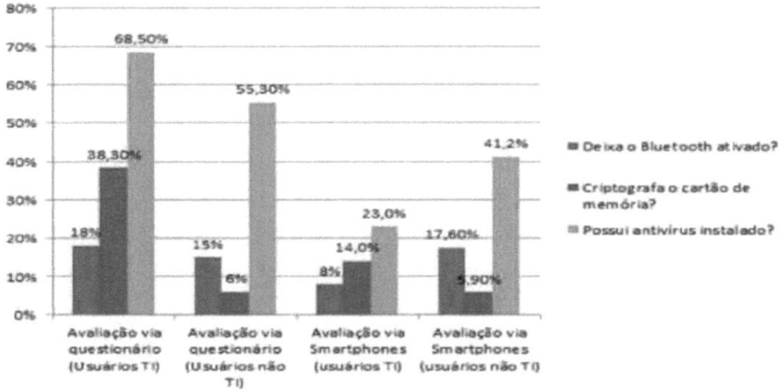


**Figure 5.3- Comparison of evaluations**

This comparison further reinforced the need for the solution proposed in this work, because, for example, 38.3 per cent of IT-savvy users say that encrypting the memory card is important, but the MSC solution showed that only 14 per cent do so.

Another interesting fact is that 68.5 per cent of these users say that it is important to have an antivirus installed and the application showed that, in practice, only 23 per cent have an antivirus installed. In the case of users without IT knowledge, 55.3 per cent say that it is necessary to have an antivirus installed, but the MSC solution showed that only 41.2 per cent have an antivirus installed.

The solution proposed in this work, the MSC, acts directly on this problem, as it points out to the user which problems are actually on the *smartphone* at that moment, and which the user has often forgotten or chosen not to configure correctly, even though they are aware that such configuration can lead to security risks.

## 5.4 EVALUATION OF THE ENERGY CONSUMPTION OF THE MSC SOLUTION

This evaluation consists of showing the level of energy consumption of the MSC solution. The concern in making this analysis is to provide an energy-efficient solution, especially when the same application suggests that the user only use applications with energy consumption compatible with their purpose.

The evaluation took place as follows: the MSC solution was installed on 10 *smartphones* of different brands and, in order to measure the energy level of the MSC solution on the *smartphones,* the *Battery Doctor* app [Cheetah 2016] was installed. This app is an energy manager that measures consumption and increases battery life, and contains a ranking of apps with high battery power consumption [Mobile, 2016]. It's worth noting that even if the *Android* operating system is configured with the "battery" option (which depends on its version), it's still not enough to make a complete energy measurement of all installed applications, as this feature only evaluates the main applications with high consumption and resources from the *Android* operating system itself.

*After* starting the MSC solution and leaving it in *standby* mode, an increase in the MSC solution's battery power consumption was seen, ranging from 2.08% to 2.31%. After starting the check on users' *smartphones*, consumption averaged between 4.87% and 5.03%. In order to make a comparative assessment of this consumption, a search was carried out on the application considered to have "high consumption" of energy according to the report [AVG 2015], which is a report that identifies and shows the energy consumption of applications on *Android smartphones.* According to the report, this app consumes an average of 8 per cent. Considering that MSC's energy consumption is below the app that consumes the least energy among the apps considered to be "high consumers" of energy, it can be argued that MSC's consumption is within a satisfactory consumption standard.

## 5.5 FINAL CONSIDERATIONS

The main objective of this chapter is to evaluate the solution proposed in this work, the MSC. To do this, the *smartphones of* two groups of users were checked for possible insecure settings, and the solution was able to detect these settings and alert users to their existence. In addition, it was seen that even the most IT-savvy users also frequently adopt insecure usage policies, which helps to further emphasise the importance of the proposed solution. Finally, the solution also showed a low percentage of battery power consumption, considering the AVG (Antivirus Guard) *Android* Application Performance Report [AVG 2015], which shows the applications that consume the most battery power.

**CHAPTER 6**

# CONCLUSIONS AND FUTURE WORK

The results described in this paper show that the number of security flaws in mobile device user configurations is generally relatively high, and this leads to an unwanted situation of insecurity for the user. With this in mind, this work proposed a solution for identifying insecure configurations on the mobile device, with the aim of minimising the security risks associated with using said device. To help the user with this task, the MSC (Mobile *Security Check)* application was developed, which works to improve the security settings of mobile devices based on the user's configuration decisions. Implemented on the *Android* platform, its function is to check the mobile device for possible misconfigurations based on the main references in the area of mobile device security, such as the NIST (National Institute of Standards and Technology) guidelines [Souppaya et *al* 2013], the CERT.br (Centre for the Study, Response and Treatment of Security Incidents in Brazil) [CERT.br 2013] and the booklet from the National Education and Research Network's Security Incident Response Centre [CAIS/RNP 2012]. The solution was developed in such a way that it is possible to incorporate new suggestions that arise in these or other booklets.

## 6.1 RESULTS ACHIEVED

In the context of this work, some important results have been achieved, which will be briefly described in this section.

- Provision of a solution for assessing *smartphone* security levels. The MSC solution has been available to *download* from the *Google Play* shop since 15 March 2016, and to date has approximately 300 downloads from different countries. The solution can be accessed at the following link: https://play.google.com/store/apps/details?id=com.msccheck.che ck.checker;
- Dissemination of the results of the research into the theoretical framework of this dissertation through a scientific article in a journal [Cavalcanti, 2015];
- Evaluation of the security level of *Android smartphones* based on the quality of user settings. From the results obtained in the evaluation of this work, it

can be inferred that a significant number of users do not configure their *smartphones* correctly, leading to a state of insecurity. This fact has made it all the more important to have an application that can search for misconfigurations and present them to the user;

- Finally, the implementation of the solution was registered with the NPI (National Institute of Industrial Property) under registration number BR 51 2016 001044 4 with the support of the Federal Rural University of Pernambuco.

## 6.2 FUTURE WORK

Some possible initiatives are envisaged in the future context of this work. Initially, one possible improvement would be to increase the number of security items to check for user misconfiguration. Examples of important items include, for example, checking whether the user has left social networks or e-mail connected; that is, without the need to *log in,* making the device an easy target for a malicious person to gain access to sensitive data.

Another possibility for future work is for the solution to also perform static and dynamic analysis of applications on the *Android* operating system, in addition to the existing functionalities.

- Static analysis involves checking the *software* code in its textual state, even before it is compiled, thus making it possible to examine all possible execution paths and variable values. The advantage of this type of analysis is that it improves the level of security, since it is possible to check the application code (even using reverse engineering, when only the application executable is available) in order to analyse this code and check for possible security breaches.

- Dynamic analysis acts as a complement to static analysis; it emulates the operating system or application, and is concerned with the data entered into the routine, the output of the data entered (especially whether it is what is expected), the response time, the functional behaviour and the performance of the application as a whole. Its main advantage is that it reveals subtle defects or vulnerabilities whose origins are too complex to discover in static analysis. Dynamic analysis can play an important role in trying to guarantee security, even though its main objective is to find and eliminate errors (debug) [Conviso 2015].

Another important piece of future work is to produce an English version of the MSC solution. With this, it could have a wider reach both for users themselves and for *feedback on* the solution worldwide. In short, having the application also in English could facilitate its use in other remote locations.

Another possible future initiative would be for the solution to be able to automatically configure the items that are checked if the user agrees with the recommendations. In practical terms, the user would have two options: to configure the desired items individually by clicking on each item, or by clicking on the "configure all items" button, in which all possible items for automatic configuration would be configured.

Another possibility for future work is to carry out a survey evaluating the MSC solution in information technology companies and IT professionals, so that feedback can be obtained on possible improvements to the solution and other items related to user misconfiguration.

Finally, there are also plans to develop the solution for other platforms, especially *Windows Phone* and IOS. With the adoption of other platforms, other checking items will naturally have to be evaluated and implemented, allowing the solution to be more complete and used by a wider range of users.

CHAPTER 7

# REFERENCES


**[Android 2016]** S. Android. **Welcome to the Android Open Source Project!** Available at https://source.android.com/. Accessed on 31/08/2016.

**[Alliance** 2016]A//ance. O, *Handset.* Available at http://www.openhandsetalliance.com/. Accessed on 30/08/2016.

**[AV- TEST 2016]AV- TEST. The best antivirus software for *Android.*** Available at https://www.av-test.org/en/antivirus/mobile-devices/. Accessed on 15/04/2016.

**[AVG** 2015]AVG. **What is Malware?** Available at http://www.avg.eom/a/br-pt/what-is-malware. Accessed on 16/05/2016.

**[AVG** 2015]AVG. What is Spyware? Available at http://www.avg.eom/a/br-pt/what-is-spyware. Accessed on 17/05/2016.

**[Anti-Malware 2016] A,** Malwarebytes. Malwarebytes Anti-Malware. Available at https://play.google.com/store/apps/details?id=org.malwarebytes.antimalware &hl=en_BR. Accessed on 20/08/2016. **[Braga 2012]** Braga, A. M. , Nascimento, E. N., Palma, L. R. and Rosa, R. **P.Introduction to Modern Mobile Device Security - An *Android* Case Study. Minicourses of the XII Brazilian Symposium on Information and Computer Systems Security,** SBSeg 2012. Available at http://wiki. inf.ufpr.br/maziero/lib/exe/fetch. php?media=ceseg:2012-sbseg- mc2.pdf. Accessed on 19/04/2016.

**[CAIS/RNP** 2012JCAIS/RNP. **Mobile Device Security Primer.** Available at http://www.enq.ufrgs.br/files/Cartilha_de_Seguranca_em_Dispositivos_Mov eis.pdf. Accessed on 31/05/2016.

**[Canaltech 2014]** Canaltech. **Ransomware attacks on mobile devices are increasing in Brazil.** Available at: http://canaltech.com.br/noticia/seguranca/Ataques-do-tipo-ransomware-a- dispositivos-moveis-sao-cada-vez-maiores-no-Brasil/. Accessed on: 20/04/2016.

**[Cavalcanti 2015]** Cavalcanti, k., Viana, E. and Lins, F. **Security Issues and Solutions for *Android* -based Mobile Devices.**nternational Journal of Computer Science and Information Security (IJCSIS), Vol. 13, No. 9, September 2015.

**[CERT.br 2003]** CERT.br. **Security Practices for Internet Network Administrators.** Available at http://www.cert.br/docs/seg-adm- redes/seg-adm-redes.html. Accessed on 01/09/2016.

**[CERT.br 2012]** CERT.br. **Security on mobile devices.** Available at http://cartilha.cert.br/dispositivos-moveis. Accessed on 20/02/2016.

**[CIS 2016]** CIS, **Centre for Internet Security.** Security benchmarks. Available at https://benchmarks.cisecurity.org. Accessed on: 22/08/2016.

**[check 2016]** M, Security Check. **Mobile Security Check.** Available at https://play.google.com/store/apps/details?id=com.msccheck.check.checker. Accessed on 30/08/2016.

**[Cheetah** 2016]Cheetah, M. Inc. **Battery Doctor.** Available at https://play.google.com/store/apps/details?id=com.ijinshan.kbatterydoctor_e n&hl=en_BR. Accessed on 06/07/2016.

**[Cheetah** 2016]Cheetah, M. **Clean Master (Optimiser).** Available at https://play.google.com/store/apps/details?id=com.cleanmaster.mguard. Accessed on 27/07/2016.

**[Conviso 2015]** Conviso. **Understand the differences between dynamic and static application testing.** Available at http://blog.conviso.com.br/entenda-as-diferencas-entre-testes-de- dynamic-and-static-applications/. Accessed on: 15/07/2016.

**[D'ARCY** 2011]D'arcy, Paul. MARKETING, Large Enterprise. CIO **Strategies for Consumerisation: the Future of Enterprise Mobile Computing.** 2011. Available at http://www.au- kbc.org/bpmain1/Security/enterprise_mobile_computing.pdf. Accessed on 15/06/2016.

**[Dermartine 2013]** D. Felipe. **WEP, WPA, WPA2: what do the acronyms mean for your WiFi?** Available at http://www.tecmundo.com.br/wi-fi/42024-wep-wpa-wpa2-o-que-as-siglas- mean-for-your-wifi-.htm. Accessed on 01/09/2016.

**[Dormann 2014]** Dormann, W. **Vulnerability Note Database.** Available at https://www.kb.cert.org/vuls/id/582497. Accessed on 28/03/2016.

[Grossmann 2015]Grossmann, L.O. **Brasill is the seventh country in the global Internet usage raking.** Available at http://convergenciadigital.uol.com.br/cgi/cgilua.exe/sys/start.htm7UserActive Template=site&infoid=39200&sid=4#.VRAQ2fnF98F. Accessed on 10/02/2016.

**[Guo 2013]Guo,** M. Bhattacharya, P. Yan, M, Qian, K and Yang, L. **Learning mobile security with *Android* security labware.** Proceeding of the 44th ACM technical symposioum on Computer Science education March 2013, Pages 675-680.

**[IBM 2008]IBM** Software Group. **Minimising code defects to improve software quality and lower development costs.** IBM Rational Software Analyzer and IBM Rational PurifyPlus software. October 2008.

**[PMBOK 2014]** PMBOK. PMI Standards Committee. A Guide to the Project Management Body Knowledge 2014, PMI Publishing Division, Philadelphia, USA.

**[Jeter 2013]** Jeter, L., and Shivakant, M. **"Identifying and quantifying the *Android* device users' security risk exposure."** Computing, Networking and Communications (ICNC), 2013 International Conference on 28 Jan. 2013: 11-17.

**[Mimoso 2016]** Mimoso, Michael. **Scanner Finds Malicious *Android* Apps at Scale.** Available at https://threatpost.com/scanner-finds- malicious-Andro/d -apps-at-scale/114438/. Accessed on 22/05/2016.

**[Mobile 2016]** Mobile, AVG. **Free Antivirus for *Android.*** Available at https://play.google.com/store/apps/details?id=com.antivirus. Accessed on 27/07/2016.

**[Novaes 2014]** Novaes, Rafael. **Learn how to recognise and remove fake APPs from *Android* .** Available at http://www.psafe.com/blog/saiba-como- recognise-remove-fake-apps-Andro/d /. Accessed on **20/06/2016.**

**[Oracle 2016]** Oracle. **Java SE Development Kit 7 Downloads.** Available at http://www.oracle.com/technetwork/pt/java/javase/downloads/jdk7- downloads-1880260.html.html. Accessed on 22/08/2016.

**[Overflow** 2015]S. Overflow. Available at stackoverflow.com. Accessed on 21/07/2016.

**[Play 2016]** P, Google. **Google Play.** Available at https://play.google.com/store?hl=pt_BR. Accessed on 20/08/2016

**[Player** 2016]Flash, **Adobe Player.** Available at http://www.adobe.com/br/products/flashplayer.html. Accessed on 20/08/2016.

**[Qualcomm** 2015]Qualcomm, C. Experiences, **Inc. Snapdragon™BatteryGuru** . Available at https://play.google.com/store/apps/details?id=com.xiam.snapdragon.app&hl =en_BR. Accessed on 19/07/2016.

**[Roberts 2014]** Roberts, J. AVG. **AVG *Android* App Performance Report Q4 2014 *Android.*** Available at http://now.avg.com/avg-Andro/d -app-performance-report-q4-2014-presskit/. Accessed 07/07/2016.

**[Romer 2015]R. Brazil concentrates 92 per cent of ransomware cases in Latin America. America.** Available at http://corporate.canaltech.com.br/noticia/protecao-de-dados/brasil- concentra-92-dos-casos-de-ransomware-na-america-latina-48259/. Accessed on 16/03/2016.

**[Salutes 2016]** B. Salutes. **How to back up Android: say goodbye to file loss!** Available at http://www.androidpit.com.br/backup-android. Accessed on 01/09/2016.

**[Serowy** 2015]Serowy, S. **Apps that consume the most of your mobile phone's battery and data plan.** Available at http://www.Andro/dpit.com.br/aplicativos-que-mais-consomem-bateria-dados. Accessed on 29/03/2016.

**[Souppaya *et al*** 2013]Souppaya, M. and Scarfone, K. **Guidelines for Managing the Security of Mobile Devices in the Enterprise.** Available at http://nvlpubs.nist.gov/nistpubs/SpecialPublications/NIST.SP.800- 124r1.pdf. Accessed on 15/06/2016.

**[Soares** 2014]Soares, D. **How to Visualise Apps and Services that Expend the Most Battery.** Available at http://www. escola Andro/d .com/como- visualizar-gasto-de-bateria/. Accessed on 05/07/2016.

**[Storm** 2016]Storm, D. **98% of *Malware* Targets the *Android* Platform.** Available at http://www.computerworld.com/article/2475964/. Accessed on 19/03/2016.

[Studio 2015]Studio, D. App. **DU Battery Saver.** Available at https://play.google.com/store/apps/details?id=com.dianxinos.dxbs&hl=p_BR. Accessed on 19/07/2016.

**[Studio 2016]** Studio, A. ***Android* Studio.** Available at https://developer.Andro/d .com/studio/index.html. Accessed on 21/08/2016.

**[Vecchiato** 2015]Vecchiato, D, Vieira, M and Martins, L. **A security configuration assessment for *Android* devices.** Proceedings of the 30th Annual ACM Symposium on Applied Computing April 2015.

**[Xdadevelopers 2015]** Xdadevelopers. **Forum.xda-developers.** Available at forum.xda-developers.com. Accessed on: 21/07/2016.

**[Zefferer** 2013]Zefferer, T. and Teufl , P. **Policy-based Security Assessment of**

**Mobile End-User Devices An Alternative to Mobile**

**Device Management Solutions for *Android* Smartphones .** Conference on 2013 International, 29-31 July 2013.

**[ZhouY 2012]Zhou** and X. Jiang.Dissecting *Android* malware: **Characterisation and evolution.** In Security and Privacy (SP), 2012 IEEE **[Symposium 2012]** Symposium on, pages 95 -109, May 2012.

CHAPTER 8

# APPENDIX

Appendix A - MSC solution start screen.

Appendix B - Screen showing the "Help" and "About the application" menus

Appendix C - Report of the MSC solution check after installation on the *smartphones* of 25 IT users and 25 non-IT users.

Home screen with password

Unencrypted memory card

There are suspicious applications with access to SMS reading

Your anchor has a password

Your anchor has a weak password

There are suspicious applications with access to GPS

No P2P connection

There are suspicious applications with access to the diary

Bluetooth is not active

There are applications installed externally

Your WI-FI connection is secure

There are no suspicious applications

You have a recommended antivirus installed

High battery consumption

Device overloaded

You consume a lot of mobile data

Appendix D - Questions from the *Android* Security Assessment questionnaire carried out with 25 IT users and 25 non-IT users.

Do you have a computer qualification?

Which screen lock do you use on *Android?*

Encrypted memory card?

Do you share the internet with a password?

Do you use *Bluetooth* with a password?

Do you always use WI-FI with encryption?

Do you have antivirus software installed?

MIX
Papier aus verantwortungsvollen Quellen
Paper from responsible sources
FSC® C105338

Printed by Books on Demand GmbH, Norderstedt / Germany